Fast Fabulous Quilt Bindings

STEP BY STEP

by

SHIRLEY SANDOZ

Acknowledgements

The ideas in this book started with a class project at my quilt guild, Cabin Fever Quilters. The project was a table runner with a spiral shape that included inside curves, outside curves, and sharp points in the binding. As I struggled to get the binding to behave, I developed a technique that helped with the sharp corners. Several guild members asked me to "write it down" so they could remember the steps. That initial effort evolved into this book.

Anyone who writes a "how to" book builds on the work of previous authors. I have learned so much from Susan K. Cleveland, Dena Crain, Kathleen Loomis, Cody Mazuran and many others too numerous to mention. Throughout the book I have tried to give credit for especially good ideas by others. My apologies to anyone I failed to credit. Any errors in the techniques as described are my own.

Many thanks also go to my good friend Ruth Allen, who provided excellent suggestions to improve the first draft; to members of my guild Kathy Stavney, Maureen Huff, Megan Bailey-Bergstein, Paula Vanderheul and Fabienne Farley who reviewed the first proof version and found errors and much needed clarification. And to Ginny Hillsberg who told me about the Corner Seam self binding method included in Chapter VII, which motivated me to figure out how to do it. Ginny also generously volunteered her impressive editing skills to help me improve the proof copy.

<u>Dedication</u>

To the members of Cabin Fever Quilters, who generously provide enthusiasm, inspiration, and a warm, welcoming "quilting home" at every meeting.

And to Carol Miller, the co-founder and dean of Quilt University (www.quiltuniversity.com) who provides another kind of welcoming "quilting home" for quilters around the world.

Table of Contents

I. Introduction

Is binding your least favorite part of making a quilt? This book will help you quickly complete a beautiful binding for every quilt, and provide options for embellished bindings when you or the quilt demands it.

There are many ways to finish a quilt edge. Different techniques are appropriate for different quilts.

The "workhorse" of the binding world is the double fold or French binding. It is used by most quilters most of the time, for good reason. It is very durable and suitable for nearly all quilts. If applied correctly with the "flip and fold" technique, it is both quick and beautiful. It can be applied completely by machine, or with a combination of machine and hand work. If the binding should become worn, it can be replaced without damaging the rest of the quilt. This book focuses mostly on the flip and fold technique and its variations.

To ensure your bindings are always beautiful, the description of the basic binding technique provided here is very detailed, with specifics at each step to explain why your binding may be "less than perfect". The goal is to achieve a *Fast Fabulous Quilt Binding* —and for this, the details <u>do</u> matter, each step of the way.

After providing you with the basic technique for binding a quilt with square corners, detailed steps and drawings are provided for unusual shaped quilts and for variations on the basic binding in Chapters V and VI.

Edge finishing techniques other than the double fold binding are useful for many applications and are described in Chapter VII.

Chapter VIV lists books, articles and websites describing binding/finishing techniques both included and not included in this book.

II. Preparation

Prepare the Quilt

Quilt top finished? It's time for a quality check! No beautiful binding can make up for wavy edges or wonky corners. The quilt top should have square corners and lay flat. Correct any problems before quilting. Plan your quilting with the width of your binding seam allowance in mind, so that no parts of the quilting design are hidden under the binding.

NOTE: most quilters use a ¼ inch seam allowance for attaching binding. A larger seam such as 3/8 inch can also be used. Some quilters may find it easier to sew a consistent seam allowance when it is a little wider. A wider binding is especially suitable on a larger quilt.

After quilting, square up the edges of the quilt.

*NOTE: Some quilters prefer to cut off the excess along the quilt edge **after** the binding is attached to the first side. This has a couple of advantages. The extra backing fabric makes it easier to sew evenly, especially in the corners. Also, the backing and batting can be cut slightly larger than the binding seam allowance, providing a nicely filled binding. This may*

be needed if you use a fairly wide binding strip (say 2 ½ inches) and a narrow seam allowance (1/4 inch). The disadvantage is the time to complete the extra step. You will need to mark the squared up edge of the quilt so you can line up the raw edge of the binding with it instead of with the cut edge.

An optional step: To prevent the quilt layers from shifting as you sew on your binding, baste the quilt top very close to the edge by hand or machine. If sewing by machine, use a walking or even feed foot. Sew around the entire quilt edge within the seam allowance, catching all layers with either a straight or a long narrow zigzag stitch. Avoid stretching the edge as you sew.

NOTE: If you do not have a walking foot, this basting can be done by hand instead. A walking foot makes binding application (and many other tasks) much easier, and is well worth the investment.

Plan and prepare the binding

You can make a "flip and fold" binding most any width you want, although bindings wider than about one inch (finished) might need some stitching in the middle to stabilize them. They also consume much more fabric than narrower bindings. Some quilters make their bindings 1/8th inch wide for miniature quilts, and 1/16th inch width is actually possible (see Narrow Bindings for Miniatures and Small Projects in Chapter

VIV). These narrow bindings require a slightly different technique, explained in the reference.

NOTE: Double fold quilt binding is applied in two steps. First, you sew the raw edge of the binding to one side (that is, the front or the back) of your quilt. The raw edge is sewn by machine. After you sew the raw edge, the folded edge is flipped to the second side of your quilt and sewn either by hand or machine. The first side can be either the front or the back.

Throughout Chapters II through VI, I use the terms "first side" and "second side" rather than "front" or "back" when describing the side of the quilt where the binding is to be applied. When finishing the second (folded) binding edge by hand, most quilters will apply the binding first to the front of the quilt, then hand sew the binding folded edge down on the back of the quilt. For a binding applied completely by machine, most quilters will apply the binding to the back of the quilt first, then sew the folded edge of the binding down on the front of the quilt, since the second edge will be the most attractive. But it is quilter's choice which to do first.

When finished, the binding can be wider on the second side than on the first if you wish. Don't make the second side narrower; the flip and fold corners won't work right. The following instructions for determining the binding width assume you want the binding the same width on both the front and back of your quilt; just remember that you can make the second side any size you want. For competition purposes, the judges will probably expect the binding to be the same width on both sides.

The "right" width of the fabric strip you cut for your binding depends upon the thickness of your quilt, the width of your seam allowance, and your personal preference.

1. <u>Determine the width of your binding</u> by making a test sample. Cut a 4 inch long strip of binding the width you want. For example, for a narrow binding this might be a 2 inch wide strip. Press this strip in half lengthwise, wrong sides together. Lay the strip on your quilt edge with raw edges of the binding lined up with the raw edges of the quilt as shown on the left in Figure 1. Using your sewing machine, sew the binding to the quilt with a long basting stitch, using the seam allowance width you prefer.

REALLY IMPORTANT NOTE: The actual width of your seam allowance is not important. But consistency of the width is important, as it is in accurate piecing. Practice until you get consistent results.

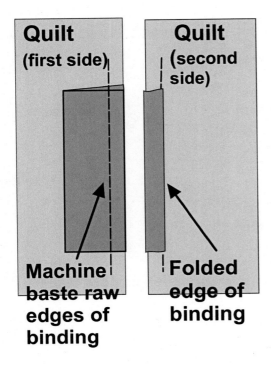

Quilt (first side)

Quilt (second side)

Machine baste raw edges of binding

Folded edge of binding

Figure 1

After sewing, fold the binding snugly around the quilt edge so the binding is "filled". The binding fold should land just beyond the stitched seam as shown on the right in Figure 1, completely covering the stitched seam.

NOTE: If you intend to sew the second side of your binding by machine, you will wish to widen the binding strip by ¼ to ½ inch. When folded, the edge will be 1/8 to ¼ inch beyond the "first side" seam. The second side stitching will then be away from the folded seam, making the stitching process easier, as will be explained later in step 25B on page 17.

Rip out the basting stitches to remove the test strip from your quilt. If the width was not right, cut a new strip and repeat the process, changing the binding strip width and/or the size of the seam allowance until you are satisfied.

2. <u>Determine the binding length and yardage.</u> The length of binding is the length of the entire outside perimeter of the quilt plus a margin for the joining seams. The method for calculating the number of strips needed for straight binding cut across the width of the fabric is:

    i. Measure the outside perimeter of your quilt in inches.

    ii. Add 18 inches to the number.

    iii. Divide by 36 (this assumes 40 inch wide fabric and allows for the joining seams).

    iv. Round up to the next whole number.

As an example, if your quilt is 42 inches wide and 50 inches long, the calculation will be as follows:

    i. Outside perimeter is 42 +42+50+50 equals 184 inches.

    ii. Add 18 to 184 equals 202 inches.

    iii. Divide 202 by 36 equals 5.61.

    iv. Round up to 6, so you will cut six strips of fabric. If the binding strips are 2 inches wide, this will require 6 times 2 inches equals 12 inches of fabric, or one third of a yard.

Should you use binding cut on the bias instead of straight of grain? Some quilters believe bias binding is more durable since there will be less wear to individual threads in the fabric. Others disagree. On a quilt with rectangular edges, I use a straight of grain binding because it is faster and easier.

Bias binding can be used any time, but is absolutely required for quilts with curved edges, such as scallops. It also can provide a nice accent if a striped fabric is used as shown in Figure 2.

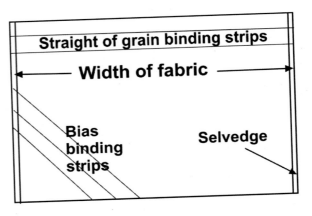

Figure 3

The following steps are the same for both straight grain and bias binding.

3. Cut your binding strips across the width of the fabric or on the bias.

4. Sew the binding strips together into one long strip using diagonal seams where the strips are joined, as shown in Figure 4. It may help to draw a diagonal line from corner to corner as a sewing guide.

Figure 2

The yardage requirements for bias binding are the same as straight of grain binding, but the binding is cut along the diagonal instead of across the width of the fabric, as shown in Figure 3. I start with 1/8 to ¼ yard extra fabric for bias binding so I don't have to use the shortest cut strips.

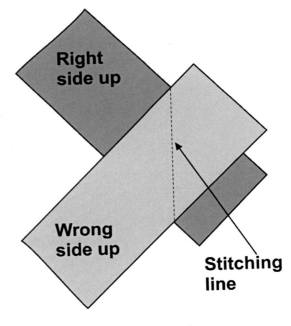

Figure 4

5. <u>Cut away the excess fabric at each join</u> leaving a ¼ inch seam allowance, as shown in Figure 5, and press the seams. You can press them to one side (a little more durable) or press open (a little less bulk).

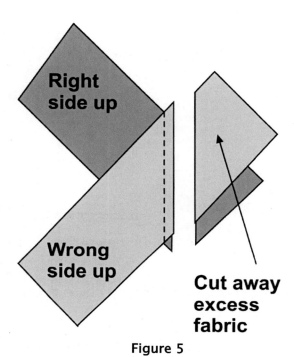

Right side up

Wrong side up

Cut away excess fabric

Figure 5

6. <u>Fold</u> the entire strip of binding in half lengthwise (wrong sides together) and press, being careful not to stretch it, especially if it is bias binding.

III. Binding Attachment – First Side

As discussed earlier, decide whether the front or the back of your quilt is the "first side".

7. <u>Position the raw edge of the binding strip</u> along the entire outside edge of your quilt. Place the start of the strip (see figure 6) in the middle of one side. If any binding seams occur at the corners of the quilt, move the starting point until there are no seams at the quilt corners. Keep the binding starting point at least 10 inches away from the first corner.

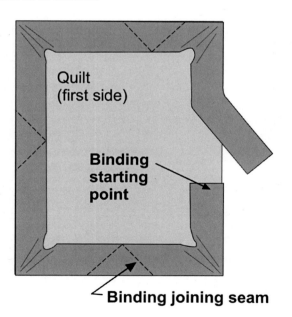

Figure 6

Once you have decided on your starting point, pin the binding down at this end.

8. <u>Sew the binding to the quilt</u> with raw edges together, leaving a ten inch length of binding at the beginning that is not attached as shown in Figure 7.

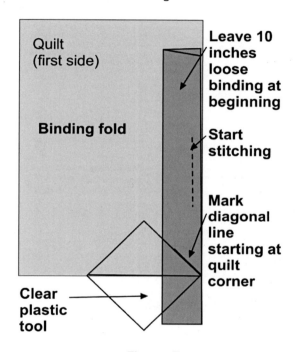

Figure 7

Stop sewing about two inches from the first corner and leave the needle down in the fabric. The next step is done with the quilt and binding still in the sewing machine.

9. <u>Mark the corner diagonal</u>. This method works best with a small tool you make out of template plastic, shown in Figure 7. The tool is just a square about three inches on a side, with a diagonal line drawn with a permanent pen across the middle. If you don't want to make such a template,

purchase a small square ruler (3 ½ inch size). The square ruler is thicker than the template plastic, so it is a little harder to use for marking the line accurately.

Position the diagonal line on the tool in line with the second raw edge of your quilt. The point of your tool must be at the corner of the quilt, but down slightly to allow for the width of the chalk or pencil line; the line should start EXACTLY at the corner. Mark the diagonal line on your quilt binding with a water soluble marker, a fine chalk pencil, or a pin.

10. <u>Resume sewing</u>, up to but not past the marked corner line as shown in Figure 8. Back stitch a few stitches. Remove the quilt from the machine, clipping threads. Add a pin at the folded edge of the binding.

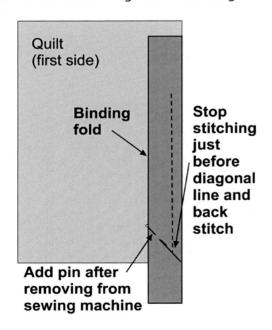

Figure 8

11. <u>Flip the binding</u>. Pin the binding to the quilt along the diagonal line near the folded edge. Flip up the binding and lay it out flat, with the binding raw edge in line with the second quilt edge as shown in Figure 9.

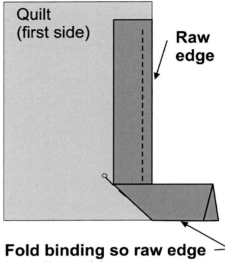

Fold binding so raw edge is in line with next quilt raw edge

Figure 9

12. <u>Fold the binding</u> back on itself over the second edge, lining up the fold exactly with the first edge as shown in Figure 10. Pin to keep the fold in position.

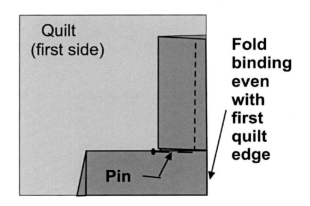

Figure 10

Turn the corner over and look at the reverse side. Is the fold exactly even with the both quilt edges? If not, adjust it and pin again.

Place a straight edge along the seam line on the first quilt edge, over the folded binding. Mark the starting point on the second edge in line with the previous seam line as shown in Figure 11.

Now you have a decision to make. You can either leave the first ¼ inch of the folded edge unstitched (as shown in Figure 11) or you can backstitch all the way to the first edge. If you do not sew to the edge, you will be able to flip the folded edge in either direction as you finish the second edge of the binding, allowing extra flexibility. You will want to have the bulk of the fold go to one side on the front of the quilt and to the other side on the back of the quilt. This makes the nicest looking corner. Depending upon which way you hand sew the second edge, the direction of the fold may make your sewing a little easier. I am left-handed, and do my hand sewing with the binding close to me and the quilt away from me. For me, that means the corners fold perfectly when the "second edge" stitching shown in Figure 11 starts at the edge. I don't need the flexibility of folding the corner either direction. So I don't leave the corner fold loose. For the rest of this chapter, we will assume you want to leave the corner fold loose.

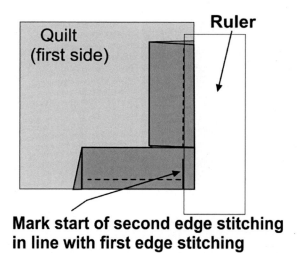

Mark start of second edge stitching in line with first edge stitching

Figure 11

13. Sew the binding to the second quilt edge. Position your needle on the stitching line about 3/8 inch away from the corner binding fold. Backstitch to the marked starting point and then sew forward. Sew past the corner about ten inches, then stop sewing with the needle down.

14. Check the quality by turning over the corner you just completed and inspecting the stitching. Make sure the stitching on both sides comes close together but doesn't overlap, as shown in Figure 12. (If you chose to sew up to the binding fold like I do, the vertical stitching line will continue down beyond the horizontal stitching line; that is okay as long as the horizontal line comes up to the vertical line but doesn't cross it).

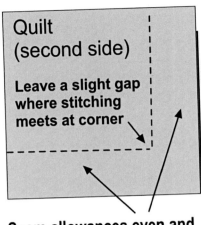

Figure 12

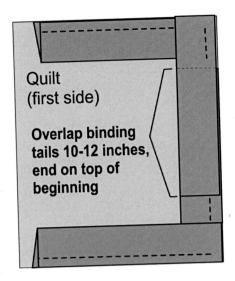

Figure 13

15. <u>Continue sewing around the quilt</u>, repeating steps 9 through 14 at each corner. As you approach the starting point, stop sewing about 12 inches before you reach the beginning of the binding stitching. The unstitched section MUST be at least two inches bigger than the width of your initial cut binding strip. The bigger this section the easier it will be to join the binding ends, so be generous unless the quilt is very small.

I learned the following technique from Cody Mazuran's book, <u>A Fine Finish</u> (Reference 1). I think it is by far the best way to join binding ends.

16. <u>Overlap the binding ends</u> as shown in Figure 13, cutting away any excess binding length beyond the unstitched area, but retaining 6–12 inches of loose binding on each end.

17. <u>Cut a small notch</u> in the middle of your overlap about 1/8 inch deep into the raw edge of <u>all four binding layers</u> (Figure 14). DO NOT CLIP THE QUILT SANDWICH. If you are nervous about cutting into your binding seam allowance, you can mark the edges of all four layers instead. Mark on the wrong side of the fabric on the top binding piece and on the right side of the fabric on the bottom binding piece.

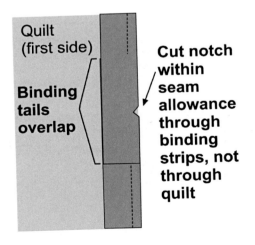

Figure 14

18. <u>Open up both ends of the binding</u> to their full width. Lay the end of your binding on top of the beginning of your binding right sides together and rotated at 90 degrees as shown in Figure 15. Be careful to avoid twisting the binding. Just open the end of the binding so the wrong side is up and open the beginning of the binding so the right side is up

NOTE: This step will be easier to manage if you take a "tuck" in the quilt sandwich underneath the unsewn section of the binding. Just make a 2 to 4 inch pleat and hold it with a couple of clothes pins until you have finished joining the binding ends.

Line up the clipped notches on the top piece with the upper left raw edge of the bottom piece, and line up the clipped notches on the bottom piece with the upper right raw edge of the top piece as shown. Pin along the diagonal line. If you need to, draw a line along the diagonal with a ruler. <u>Do not pin at the center where the binding folds come together.</u> Remove the clothes pins you used to take a tuck in the quilt.

19. <u>Carefully refold the binding</u> and lay down on the quilt sandwich. If you have done the previous steps properly, the binding will lay flat. If not, correct before sewing.

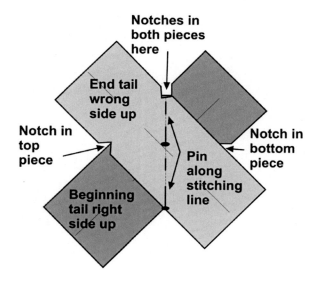

Figure 15

20. <u>Unfold the binding strips</u> so they look like Figure 15 again and then sew the two ends together along the line you pinned. Trim away the excess tails leaving ¼ inch seam allowance, just the way you joined the binding strips together back in step 5. Press the seam and the binding fold.

21. <u>Pin the joined binding to the quilt top</u> with a pin at least every inch to hold all the layers together. Sew this remaining binding to the quilt, backstitching to lock your stitches at the beginning and end.

IV. Binding Attachment – Second Side

The first side is now completed. You may wish to lightly press the binding seam in preparation for attaching the second side. Then prepare your perfect corners following the next few steps. These steps result in a fully stitched mitered corner.

22. <u>Make a mark on the fold up from the seam line</u> at a distance equal to the width of the seam allowance. Draw a diagonal line on the binding as shown in Figure 16.

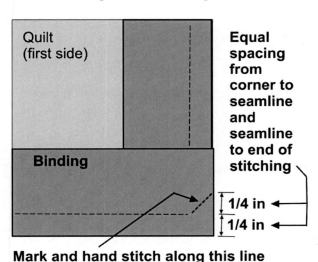

Mark and hand stitch along this line

Figure 16

23. <u>Carefully hand sew a few stitches</u> with needle and thread along the marked line in your binding. Start at the inside where the seams come together and work toward the outside fold, being careful to make tiny stitches right at the outside edge. Stitch only through the corner fold of the binding fabric; <u>do not sew through the binding seam allowance or quilt.</u> Once you have sewn all the way to the folded edge, make a good tight knot and cut your thread. The little point you have created is the outside of your binding corner, once the binding is folded over. The tiny stitches will hold the corner in a perfect point. Repeat this process for all the corners on your quilt.

24. <u>Determine the corner fold direction</u>. Before attaching the binding, you will determine which way to fold the corners. It is important that the front and back folds in the binding corner go in opposite directions to minimize bulk. Because you did not sew down the corner fold (back in step 12), you can make the folds go either way. Try both ways and see which one results in the nicest corner. If it doesn't make any difference, just choose the one that makes your folding and sewing easier. If you are sewing the folded side of the binding down by machine, pin the fold in place and follow the directions in paragraph 25B below.

NOTE: For this hand sewing, your sewing thread should match your binding rather than matching the quilt.

25A. <u>Hand sew the second side</u>.

25A.1 <u>Tack the binding to the seam allowance to control the corners.</u> If you are skilled at folded corners, you may be able to just pin the corner and avoid this little step; but try it first to see if it improves your corners.

Do this step to all four corners before you start sewing down the binding folded edge, unless you are left-handed. When sewing from left to right, these stitches in the fold can be done as you go along.

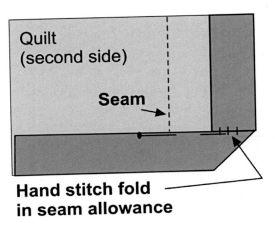

Figure 17

Fold the first side of the corner down and secure with a pin. Work completely within the seam allowance and avoid penetrating through to the binding on the other side of the quilt. Sew down the folded edge of the binding as shown in Figure 17 and knot securely. Cut your thread and repeat this process for all the corners on your quilt. Again, if you are left-handed you can do this stitching as the binding is sewn down; sewing it ahead of time is not necessary.

25A.2 <u>Sew down the binding fold</u> with a blind hem stitch.

A blind hem stitch is used so no thread shows on the surface. To sew a blind stitch, take a small horizontal stitch in the quilt just above the seam; leave a TINY gap for ease, then take a small horizontal stitch in the binding fold. Continue stitching along the entire binding fold. This is shown in Figure 18, with the separation between the quilt back and the binding fold exaggerated to let you see where to stitch. In your hem, the thread should be invisible.

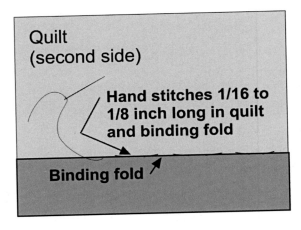

Figure 18

At each corner, sew into the seam allowance and down toward the corner as shown in Figure 19.

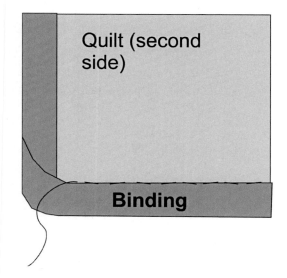

Figure 19

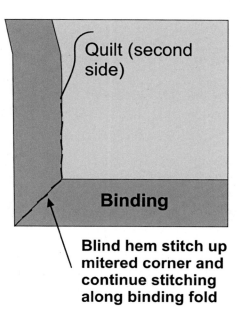

Figure 21

Then tuck the inside fold in place with a pin as shown in Figure 20 and pin the binding fold in place.

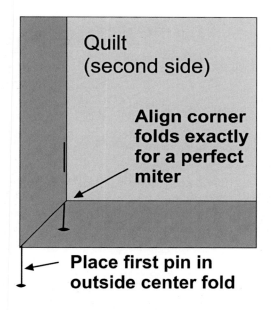

Figure 20

Sew up the corner fold as shown in Figure 21, and continue sewing the folded edge.

And here is what a fabulous finished binding looks like. Figure 22 shows the front on the left and the back on the right.

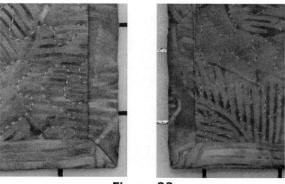

Figure 22

25B. <u>Machine sewing the second side</u>. This method can be faster than the hand sewing method, but leaves a visible line of stitching on both sides. An attractive result depends upon careful matching of the thread colors to the fabrics, careful pinning, and straight stitching.

Cut the binding strips ¼ to ½ inch wider than you would for the hand attachment method. All other binding preparation steps in Chapter II are the same. The "first side" binding attachment is usually done on the back of the quilt. The "second side" sewing is then done on the front of the quilt.

NOTE: Use a top thread that matches your binding. Use thread that matches the first side of your quilt for the bobbin.

25B.1. <u>Try a test piece with scraps</u>. The goal is to stitch a consistent distance from the folded binding edge on the top, and have the bobbin stitching be on the quilt near the quilt binding – no more than 1/8 inch away. This is not easy. Test first with a sample quilt sandwich and binding to see if you get good results. Attach binding to the first side of your sample quilt as instructed in Chapter III. Following steps 25B.2 and 25B.3, attach binding to the second side of your quilt.

When you are happy with your practice piece and confident with your skills, go back to your quilt.

25B.2. <u>Position the binding fold</u>. Fold the binding over to the second side of the quilt and carefully pin the entire binding fold in place. Pin parallel to the stitching line. Once the pins are in place, turn the quilt over and check that the pins are all a consistent distance from the binding on the back. Adjust any pins as needed. When you

get to the corner, pin the miter in the corner carefully.

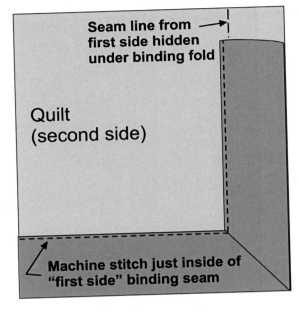

Figure 23

25B.3. <u>Sew the fold down</u>. Sew the binding fold down, about 1/16th inch away from the fold as shown in Figure 23. Start sewing in the middle of one side of the quilt, removing the pins as you sew. Stop sewing right at the corner miter, rotate the quilt 90 degrees, and continue sewing along the second edge. Continue to the beginning of your stitching. Backstitch or lock your stitches. A narrow decorative stitch, if your machine has one, may be used to sew down the binding. These stitches can disguise any small variations in alignment.

Those are all the basic steps for applying a "flip and fold" binding. Be sure to master these basic steps before proceeding to the more difficult bindings in the following chapters.

V. Special Corners and Curves

In this chapter the steps are numbered to correspond to the basic steps described earlier. Only steps that are different from the basics are described in this chapter. The step numbers in this section have a letter in front to indicate the type: C for curves, SC for sharp corner, and IC for inside corner.

Consider the shape of your quilt when preparing the binding strips. If you have a quilt with scalloped edges, you may be unable to keep all the binding joining seams out of the corners. In this instance, press the binding seams open before pressing the binding in half lengthwise, and trim the seam allowances to a generous 1/8 inch.

Curves

Curves are easy! Using a narrow bias binding is essential so the binding eases and lays flat in the curves.

When using a bias binding, do not stretch the fabric as you press the lengthwise fold and as you sew it to your quilt. That way, you "save" the stretch for the places where you need it in the curves.

The narrow width ensures you have just the right amount of binding to fold over and cover the seam line.

C1. Sew a test piece with scraps before you work on your quilt. Make a small quilt sandwich using the same fabrics and batting as your finished quilt. Cut a curve on the edge similar to the ones in your quilt. Make a short test strip of bias binding (cut a 2 inch wide strip for a ¼ inch seam allowance), press in half lengthwise and sew the binding around the curve. Fold it over the quilt edge and pin into place. If it just covers the seam line, you have the right width strip. If it doesn't cover, cut the binding a bit wider and try again. If it goes over beyond the seam line too much, make the binding a bit narrower and try again.

Once the width is right, pin the second edge of the binding in place and examine it carefully.

Inside Curve. For an inside curve, the binding should be smooth with no wrinkles on the outside edge. If you see wrinkles, remove the binding and reapply, stretching the binding slightly as you sew it.

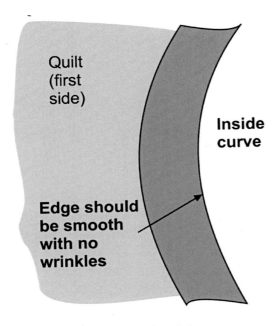

Figure 24

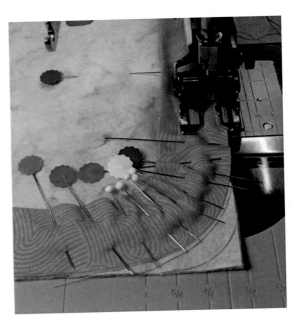

Figure 25

The finished binding for this curve is shown in Figure 26. The quilt and the binding are completely flat and wrinkle free. It does not roll either up or down.

Outside Curve. Make sure the edge has enough ease and lays flat. This will be hard to determine with the fold pinned. Sew the binding fold down over the quilt edge by hand and remove the pins. If the edge tends to roll up or down a little, then do another sample but ease more fullness in the binding as you sew down the first edge. For a very tight curve, pin the binding to the quilt (first side) carefully before sewing. Figure 25 shows a rounded quilt corner with a tight radius. The curve has been marked and the quilt left square until after binding application. Pin about every ¼ inch, removing the pins as you sew.

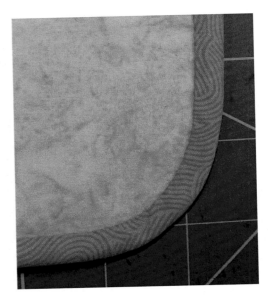

Figure 26

C8-21. <u>Sew the first side of the binding</u> according to the instructions in steps 8-21 on pages 9–13, gently easing the curves if needed.

C25A. <u>Hand sewing the second side.</u>

Pin the fold in place before sewing. When hand sewing the second side, keep the binding fold aligned perpendicular to the edge of the quilt and use the stretch in the bias binding to ease any extra fullness in (for an outside curve) or accommodate the extra length needed (for an inside curve).

C25B. <u>Machine sewing the second side.</u>

The stretch in the bias binding makes machine sewing the second side tricky. Be sure to pin very carefully, removing the pins as you sew. This is not a method I recommend for curves, since the extra width needed for a good machine binding application conflicts with the narrow width that makes bias binding easier to apply.

Sharp Outside Corners

Sharp corners are constructed the same way as the 90 degree corners shown in Chapter III, except that you do not sew as far into the corner when applying the binding.

NOTE: Make life easy on yourself—don't design a quilt with binding and corners sharper than 45 degrees! Use one of the other edge treatments described in Chapter VII.

SC8. <u>Sew the first edge of the binding.</u> Referring back to step 8 on page 9, stop stitching about 4 inches from the

corner instead of just 2 inches as recommended for a 90 degree corner. Using a small ruler, place a convenient vertical line on the ruler exactly over the point of the corner. Then rotate the ruler until the distance from that vertical line along the top of the ruler to each side of the quilt is the same, as shown in Figure 27.

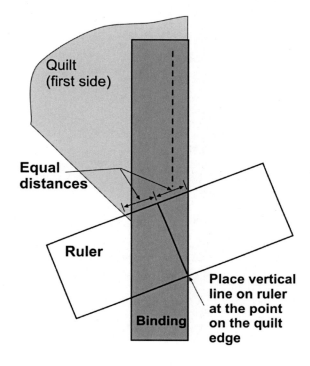

Figure 27

SC9. <u>Mark the vertical line</u> above the ruler with a pin, then line up the edge of the ruler from the pin to the corner point and draw a short line on the binding as shown in Figure 28.

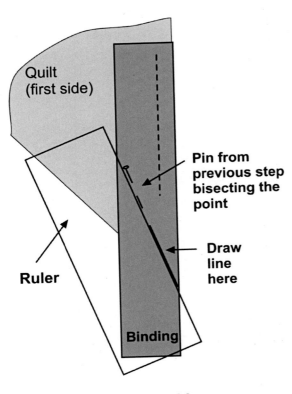

Figure 28

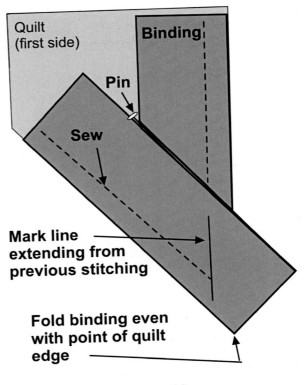

Figure 29

SC10. <u>Resume sewing</u> until you reach this line but do not cross it, then backstitch and remove your work from the sewing machine.

SC11. <u>Flip the binding</u> as in step 11 on page 10, lining the raw edge of the binding up with the second edge of the quilt as shown in Figure 32.

SC12. <u>Fold the binding</u> as in step 12 on page 10. The corner fold must start at the point as shown in Figure 29.

SC13. <u>Draw a line</u> on the binding that extends down in line with the previous stitching.

Stitch the binding to the second quilt edge. Start stitching a couple of stitch lengths away from the marked line. Backstitch to the line and then go forward about ten inches. Stop stitching with the needle down in the fabric.

NOTE: If the point on your quilt edge tends to be pushed down through your sewing machine throat plate by the needle, either switch to a straight stitch throat plate (if you have one), or put a piece of newsprint or other thin paper under the point while you stitch it. Tear away the paper after you finish stitching the corner.

SC14. <u>Check your stitching by turning the corner over to the second side.</u> The two stitching lines should end very close to each other and not overlap. The seam allowances should be consistent, as shown in Figure 30. If not, take the quilt out of the machine and fix this corner before continuing on to the next corner.

SC 15-21. <u>Complete all corners</u> and join binding at the ends following steps 15-21 on pages 12-13.

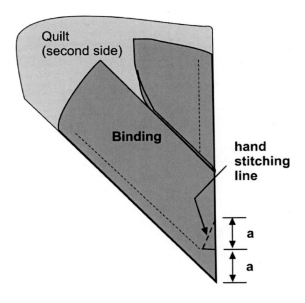

Figure 31

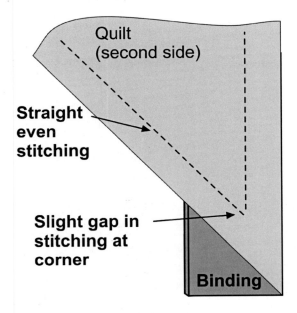

Figure 30

SC22. <u>Hand stitch the corner fold</u>. Prepare the sharp point for folding by stitching the fold as discussed in step 22 on page 14. This time the stitching line will be longer as shown in Figure 31.

Before stitching the binding down on the second side, practice turning this sharp point and pinning it in place.

There will be a lot of bulk in the point, and you may wish to trim away some of the point to minimize it, as shown in Figure 32.

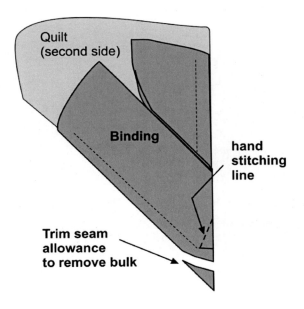

Figure 32

SC 23-25A. <u>Sew the binding down</u> on the second side as described in step 25A on page 15. You may stitch the corners down first, as described in that step, or stitch them down as you reach them. Carry the stitching into the corner as shown in Figure 33.

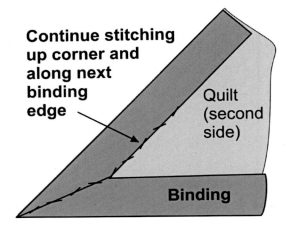

Continue stitching up corner and along next binding edge

Quilt (second side)

Binding

Figure 34

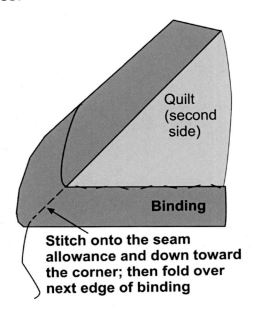

Quilt (second side)

Binding

Stitch onto the seam allowance and down toward the corner; then fold over next edge of binding

Figure 33

With the needle and thread hanging out at the point, carefully fold the second edge, tucking the corner inside the fold with a pin if necessary. Continue stitching. First stitch up the corner miter, then continue along the second binding edge. The stitches in Figure 34 show for clarity, but your stitching should be invisible as shown in the photo in Figure 35.

Inside Corners

IC6. <u>Reinforce the Inside corners.</u> After completing step 6 on page 7 and BEFORE

Figure 35

beginning the attachment of the binding, reinforce all the inside corners of the quilt sandwich and clip, as shown in Figure 36. Sew just inside the seam allowance with a short stitch length, about 15 stitches per inch. The stitching just inside the seam allowance won't show when the binding is attached. The clip should come right up to the stitching but not through it.

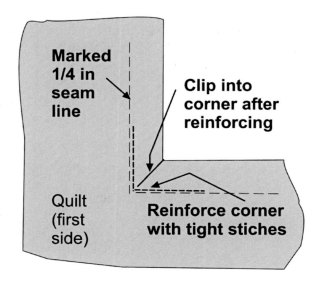

Figure 36

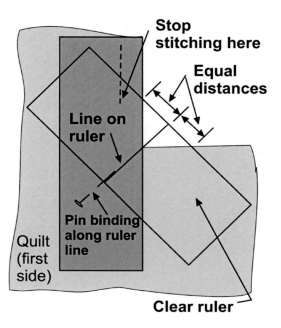

Figure 37

It is important that the reinforcing stitching and the seam allowance be positioned precisely for these inside corners to be successful. Do a couple of practice pieces before attempting a quilt.

IC7. Sew binding to the first side. Once the inside corners are reinforced and clipped, attach the first side of the binding. Proceed as directed in steps 7 and 8 on page 9, and stop stitching about 2 inches from the inside corner as shown in Figure 37.

IC8. Mark the corner as shown in Figure 37. Use a ruler to measure equal distances from each side of the corner. Place a pin at the end of the ruler line that bisects the corner. Once the pin is in place, move the ruler to draw a line on the binding between the pin and the corner.

IC9. Sew to the marked corner as shown in Figure 38.

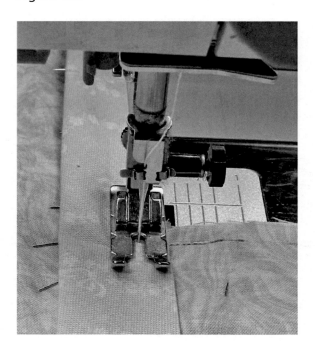

Figure 38

Stop with the needle down at the exact corner, and rotate the quilt underneath the binding so you can sew the next edge. Make a big triangular pleat in the quilt at the corner as shown in Figure 39, and also in the photo in Figure 40.

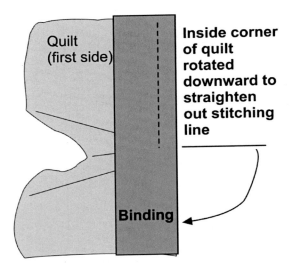

Figure 39

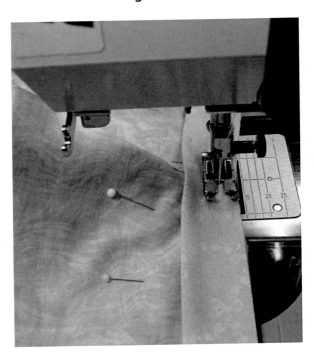

Figure 40

IC10 and 11. <u>Continue sewing past the corner</u>. When you are certain the layers of

quilt and binding are flat under the needle with no pleats or tucks, sew the next quilt edge. After you are several inches past the inside corner you just completed, stop sewing with needle down and flip the corner over to check the second side. If the corner isn't right, stop and fix any problems now. If necessary, rip out your stitching back to the corner and sew again. The binding will stand up in the corner as shown in Figure 41.

Figure 41

IC12–21. <u>Continue sewing around the perimeter</u> of the quilt and join the ends as instructed in steps 12 through 21 on pages 10–13. Do a final check of all the corners and make sure any curves lay flat when the binding is sewn down.

Once you are satisfied with the binding first side application, you are ready to sew down the second side of the binding by hand. Prepare any square corners as described in step 22 and 23 on page 15 or sharp points as described in step SC22 on page 23.

IC22. <u>Prepare the inside corner tuck</u>. For an inside corner, the binding is longer at the seam than at the outside quilt edge. This extra length is about twice the width of the binding seam allowance. This extra length must be tucked under in the corner. The next few paragraphs show how to mark the size and shape of the tuck and how to sew it.

Mark a horizontal line on the binding starting at the corner seam (hidden under the binding in Figure 42).

For a 90 degree inside corner, measure the actual width of the binding between the stitched seam and the fold. Mark a vertical line along the binding at the half way point as shown in Figure 42.

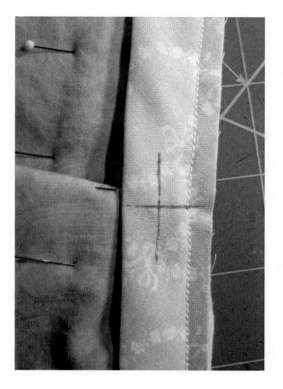

Figure 42

Now fold the binding along the horizontal line coming out from the corner and the quilt along a diagonal line starting from the corner as shown in Figure 43 and the photo in Figure 44. Place your corner marking tool or a small ruler as shown in Figure 43 and mark the two diagonal stitching lines.

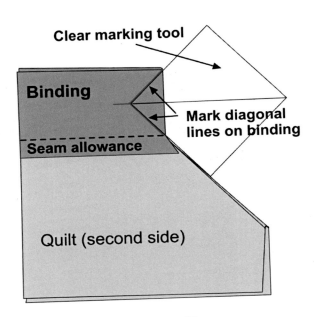

Figure 43

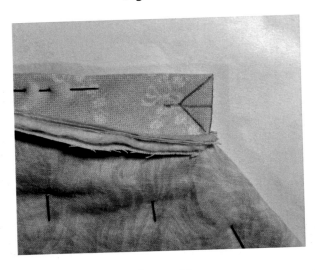

Figure 44

Stitch the tuck along the little corner you have just marked with very small stitches, catching all the layers of the binding but not the quilt.

Test the corner by folding over the binding; if necessary trim the seam allowance (NOT the binding) to reduce bulk. It is also possible to cut away the center of the

binding tuck as shown in Figure 45. Do this only if necessary to get the corner to lie flat, and be cautious about how much you cut away.

Figure 45

When all inside corners have been tucked in this manner, you are ready to apply the binding to the second side as described in step 25A on page 15.

NOTE: I don't recommend an inside corner with less than 90 degrees. For corners more than 90 degrees (more open), a little geometry is required to determine the shape of the tuck. For a 90 degree inside corner, the distance from the binding fold to the corner of the tuck seam is half the binding width (minus the seam allowance), or about 3/8 inch for a binding strip cut 2 inches with a ¼ inch seam allowance. For a 135 degree corner, the distance is 0.414 x 3/8 or 5/32 (slightly more than 1/8) inch. For a 120 degree corner, the distance is

0.58 x 3/8 or 7/32 (slightly less than ¼) inch.

IC25A. <u>Sew the binding second edge</u>. As you reach each inside corner, pin the binding fold over the seam line and hand stitch all the way to the corner. Reinforce this point with a few very tiny stitches, remove the pins and continue stitching to the next corner. It is not easy to get the corner to behave, so be persistent and use lots of pins as shown in Figure 46.

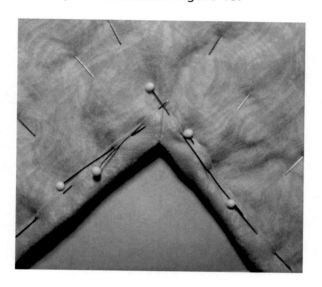

Figure 46

The finished inside corner is shown from the front on the left side of Figure 47 and from the back on the right side.

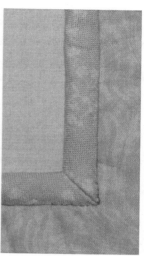

Figure 47

Special Corners and Curves – practice piece

If you have a special quilt project in mind, make a practice piece that has the corners or curves to be used in your project. If you just want to practice the techniques in this chapter, make up a scrap quilt sandwich. Figure 48 shows a practice piece that can be made from a couple of fat quarters. The exact dimensions are not important, but be generous with the size, since bigger will be easier. Pin the sandwich about every 4 inches in both directions, or machine baste across the sandwich several times to hold the layers together. Baste the edge within the seam allowance to hold all the layers together if you wish. When you reach the sharp point, slip some tissue paper or newsprint under the point to keep the fabric from going down into the throat plate. When you have finished stitching the edge, tear away the tissue paper. Then follow the instructions in this book for each type of corner or curve, evaluating your results as you go.

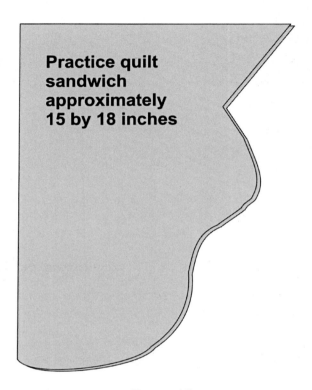

Figure 48

VI. Embellished Bindings

Embellished bindings can add a special finishing touch to your quilt. Use a striped fabric, cut on the bias. Or cut a variety of fabrics into narrow strips, piece them together on the long sides and cut your binding strips from that, either crosswise or on the diagonal. Inset piping, lace, rick rack, or prairie points between the binding and the quilt front. Each different binding in this section is labeled with EB and a number. The numbers do not correspond with the step numbers in earlier chapters.

EB1. Two-sided binding

Sometimes you would like to use a different color binding on the back of the quilt. This easy technique solves that problem. The instructions below assume that you will attach the binding first to the quilt front and then hand sew the binding fold to the back of the quilt.

Cut the binding front fabric in one inch wide strips – enough strips to go around the quilt plus 18 inches. Join the strips together with diagonal seams to form one continuous strip, as shown in step 4. Cut the binding back fabric in two inch wide strips and join into one continuous strip. Sew the two fabric strips together as shown below In Figure 49.

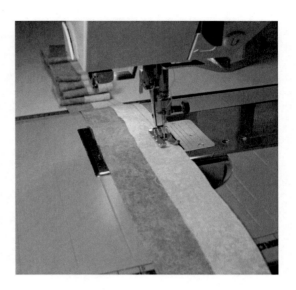

Figure 49

Press the seam allowance toward the wider fabric strip. Fold and press the binding in half lengthwise, wrong sides together.

Attach the binding to the front of the quilt with the front binding fabric down, as shown in Figure 50 below. Flip and fold the corners and join the ends as with one sided binding.

Figure 50

Fold the binding over to the back side and stitch in place by hand, being careful to keep the seam between the two fabrics right on the outer folded edge. The back side is shown as pinned before sewing in Figure 51 below.

Figure 51

The finished binding is shown from the front in Figure 52.

Figure 52

EB2. Integrated Trim Binding

I first learned this binding technique from a pattern by Barb's Elegant Designs (her website is *www.barbselegantdesigns.com)*. I love her patterns and fabrics, and this slick binding technique was an unexpected bonus! An article "Faux Piped Binding" by Trisha Chubbs also describes this method, and is listed in the references.

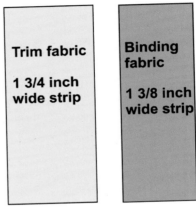

Figure 53

This binding is prepared by cutting strips of two different fabrics. The trim fabric is cut 1 ¾ inches wide. The main binding fabric is cut 1 3/8 inches wide. Join enough strips of each fabric together end to end (with diagonal seams) to go around the entire quilt plus 18 inches.

The two different fabric strips are then sewn together lengthwise as shown in Figure 54 to form the binding.

Figure 54

For a flat flange trim, press the seam toward the binding fabric, then press the whole strip in half lengthwise, wrong sides together.

NOTE: If the seam allowance is pressed toward the trim fabric, the seam allowance will add thickness to the flange, giving it a little dimension. Press carefully and inspect to ensure the seam allowance is inside the flange; it may need to be trimmed so it will lie flat.

The binding is first applied to the <u>back</u> of the quilt, with the trim fabric side facing up as shown in Figure 55 so you don't see the main binding fabric from the top. It is applied in the usual manner, flipping and folding the corners.

Figure 55

Fold the binding over to the front of the quilt and pin in place along the seam, carefully mitering each corner as shown in Figure 56. Check the locations of the pins on the back of the quilt to make sure you have folded the edge a consistent width everywhere, especially at the corners.

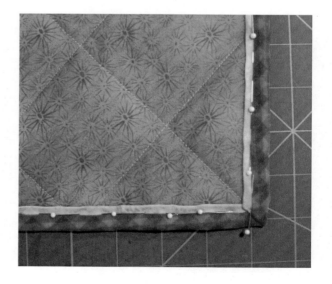

Figure 56

Sew the binding fold down by stitching in the ditch where the trim fabric meets the main binding fabric as shown in Figure 57. Use your walking foot. Select a thread color for the top that matches the trim fabric, and a bobbin thread color that matches the back of the quilt.

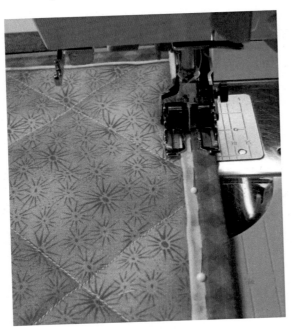

Figure 57

Figure 58 shows the finished trimmed edge.

Figure 58

EB3. Binding with outside piped edge

Cording can usually be found in the upholstery section of your local craft/fabric store. It comes in various materials and sizes. If you select cotton cording, preshrink the cording before use. This can be done by putting it in a lingerie bag and running it through your washer and dryer, or washing by hand in hot water.

Cording size used for quilt trim should be about $1/16^{th}$ to $3/32$ inch in thickness.

Before cording is used it must be transformed into piping by wrapping it with fabric. Ready-made piping is available in the section of your local sewing/craft store where the rick rack and other trims are found.

Ready-made piping comes in a few solid colors and is a cotton/poly blend. Make your own piping for the most color and fabric flexibility.

The instructions below use a zipper foot with your sewing machine. Piping feet are available for most sewing machines and can be used also. Adjust the needle position to the left until the needle operates freely on the left side of the zipper foot. For sewing machines that can't move the needle position, slide the zipper foot to the right.

To make piping, cut 1 ½ inch wide <u>bias</u> strips of your piping fabric. For outside edge piping, make one continuous strip of piping about 18 inches longer than the

34

perimeter of your quilt. Join the strips together lengthwise with diagonal seams (as for binding) and press the seams open to minimize bulk. Press the strip in half lengthwise, wrong sides together, as you would for binding.

Tuck the cording into the fold at one end and slide it under the zipper foot, making sure the cording stays snugly in the fold as shown in Figure 59. For this photograph and several following ones I am using a large cording not generally recommended for quilts. After struggling with it for this demonstration, I can't recommend it either. Use a narrower cording to make things easy.

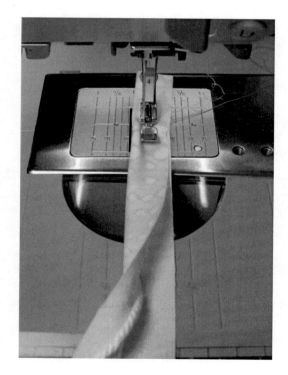

Figure 59

After completing the piping, trim the seam allowance to an exact ¼ inch. This process

can be done with any quilting ruler, but will be made much easier if you purchase a tool for this purpose, such as the Groovin' Piping Trimming Tool™, available at your local quilt shop or from the inventor, Susan K. Cleveland, at her website www.PiecesBeWithYou.com . The tool has a ½ inch seam allowance side and a ¼ inch side; use the ¼ inch side for this purpose as shown in Figure 60.

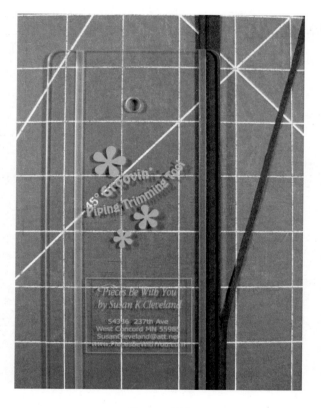

Figure 60

Note that you will also need to trim the seam allowance to ¼ inch if you are using purchased piping.

To form the binding, cut enough one inch wide and two inch wide strips from your binding fabric to go around your quilt plus

18 inches. Join the strips with diagonal seams lengthwise (as you did for the two sided binding in EB 1) and press the seams open to minimize bulk.

NOTE: if you wish, you can use different fabrics for the 1 inch and 2 inch binding strips and then a third fabric for the piping. Wouldn't that be colorful!

Join the binding strips (right sides together) and the piping at the same time, using a piping or pintuck foot as shown in Figure 61.

If you will be using a zipper foot, I recommend you attach the piping first to the wider fabric strip only. After attaching the piping to the wide strip, turn the strips over so you have the wrong side of the narrow binding strip on the bed of the sewing machine and the wrong side of the wide strip facing up. Follow the piping stitching line, stitching just to the left so your stitching is closer to the cording and the first piping stitching line will be hidden.

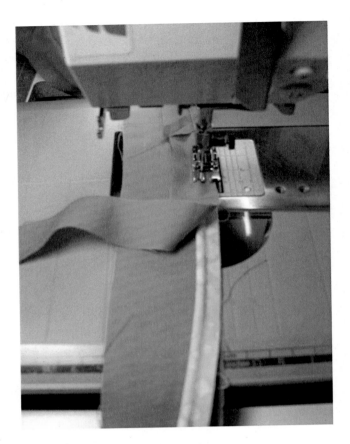

Figure 61

Carefully press the seam flat with the piping up. Then press again in half lengthwise, with the wrong sides together, resulting in the folded binding strip shown in Figure 62.

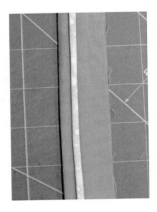

Figure 62

To attach the binding to the quilt, lay it down along the edge of the quilt top with the piping side down. Follow the usual process for attaching the binding and mitering the corners, EXCEPT make the fold at the corner a little generous. That is, instead of lining the fold up with the edge of the quilt, let the fold extend beyond the quilt edge no more than 1/16th of an inch as shown in Figure 63. This will allow a little extra ease as the binding goes around the corner.

allowance at each end as shown in Figure 64. The red lines on each end, made with a heat-sensitive marker, show the final joining line.

Figure 64

Remove the stitching that holds the piping strip in place and the initial stitching holding the cording in place, back past the final joining line, shown in Figure 65.

Figure 63

Another alternative is to round the corners and use a bias binding as shown in Chapter V on page 19-20.

After the binding is sewn around the entire quilt except for the loose tails at the beginning and end, join the ends. Joining the ends of the integrated piped binding is the trickiest part. Cut the loose tails off on the diagonal, leaving about a one inch seam

Figure 65

Then cut out the cording back to the red line on both ends and restitch the piping and the binding together as shown in Figure 66.

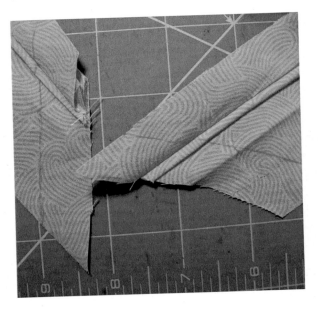

Figure 66

Pin the seam together along the red lines as shown in Figure 67.

Figure 67

The final join will be decent looking, as shown in Figure 68. How good it looks will depend on how accurately you cut back the cording and sewed the seam – yours may look better than mine!

Other techniques, such as described in Cody Mazuran's book A Fine Finish (see Chapter VIV) can provide a more reliable perfect join, but are slower because the piping is applied separately from the binding. It is your choice whether to spend the extra time for that "more perfect" result.

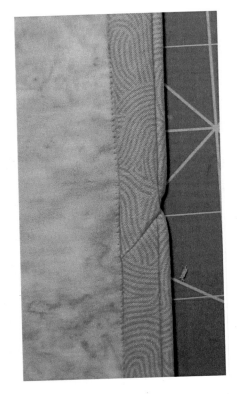

Figure 68

EB4. Prairie points

Prairie points can be added around the outside edge of the quilt or on the inside edge of the binding.

When placed on the outside edge of the quilt, binding is not required.

NOTE: leave the last couple of inches next to the quilt edge unquilted until after the prairie points are applied.

38

The points should be sewn right side down on the outside edge of the quilt top, and then the edge flipped over with the points facing out. The backing fabric seam allowance is then folded under and sewn in place by hand so that the quilt front seam allowance and all the raw edges at the base of the prairie points are enclosed. Alternatively, with careful pinning, the second edge could be sewn by machine. You can also use the "turned quilt" methods described in Chapter VII.

EB4A.   <u>**Prairie points** can be made individually or in strips.</u>   For individual prairie points, cut 2 to 4 inch squares of fabric. Pick the size you prefer to suit your quilt. As shown in Figure 69 below, prairie points can be folded in two ways. On the left both folds are on the diagonal, and result in points that can be tucked into one another, resulting in the overlapping effect shown in Figure 70.

On the right side of Figure 69, the first fold is horizontal and the second folds are diagonal. These center fold points can still be overlapped but can't be tucked into one another like the side fold points.

By using a striped fabric or alternating two fabrics, some interesting effects can be achieved with both types of folds as shown in Figure 71.

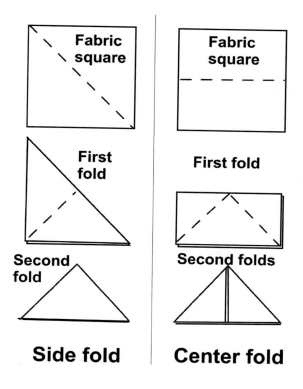

Figure 69

Figure 70

Two fabrics alternating, side fold

Striped and print fabrics, center fold

Figure 71

The lower photo shows center fold points inserted at the edge of a quilt. Alternate points are made from a striped fabric. The upper photo shows two different fabrics strip pieced with side fold points then interwoven and basted together, ready to apply to a quilt.

Single prairie points take more time to make than strip pieced points but have more flexibility. The spacing of single points can be varied, as can the fabric and size of the points. Prairie points can even be made of multiple fabrics. Piping or other trim can be inserted into the folded edge.

EB4B. Continuous strip prairie points

<u>EB4B1. Double continuous strip prairie points.</u> Cut a strip of fabric the length of the edge you wish to trim with prairie points, plus a couple of inches. The width is double the size of each prairie point plus ½ inch. For example, for a 4 inch prairie point, the width is 8 ½ inches. Press the strip in half lengthways, wrong sides together. Open the fold and do the marking in the next step on the wrong side.

Mark lines in from each long edge the same length as the prairie point size. Stagger the opposite side marks. In the 4 inch example, the left side marks are at 4, 8, 12, … inches. The right side marks are at 2, 6, 10,…inches. Cut along the lines, stopping ¼ inch away from the center fold.

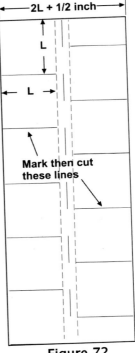

Figure 72

Fold each point along the diagonal as shown. The right side shows the fold lines on the wrong side of the fabric (It is not necessary to mark the fold). The left side shows the completed fold. Press each fold carefully.

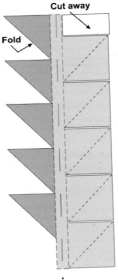

Figure 73

40

Fold the points again along the second fold line shown in the drawing. Again, press carefully. When completed, both sides will look like the left side of this drawing.

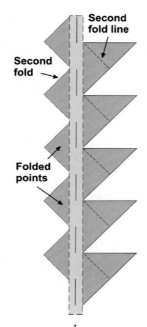

Figure 74

Press the entire strip on the center line. "Weave" the two sets of points together by pulling the flaps from one side up and over the next point. Turn the strip over and do the same thing on the other side. Both sides will appear the same.

Machine baste the points 3/8 inch from the center fold, catching all layers of fabric.

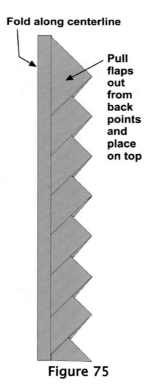

Figure 75

EB4B2. Single strip prairie points

Cut two strips of fabric the length of the edge you wish to trim with prairie points, plus a couple of inches. Both strips can be from one fabric, or two fabrics can be used as shown in the drawings here. The width or each strip is the size of each prairie point plus ½ inch. For example, for a 4 inch prairie point, the width is 4 ½ inches.

On the wrong side of the fabric, mark lines in from the right side of the strip, starting down the length of each prairie point. For example, the lines will be down 4 inches for a 4 inch prairie point. Cut along these lines, stopping ½ inch away from the left side of the strip.

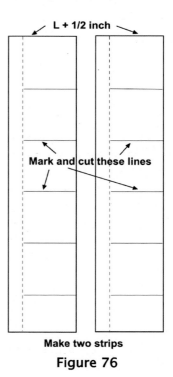

Figure 76

Fold and press along the diagonal of each point. Fold up from the lower right on one strip, and down from the upper right on the other strip. Press all folds carefully.

Figure 77

Fold and press the remaining raw edge of the folded triangle down to the ½ inch flange. Again, the folds will be in opposite directions on the two strips. The first strip (green) is folded down from the upper right. The second strip (blue) is folded up from the lower right. Press.

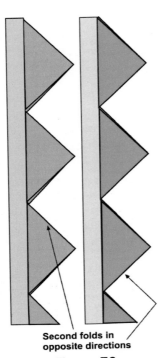

Figure 78

Place the two strips with the flanges wrong sides together with all the points folded in the same direction. Offset one strip so that the points are evenly distributed as shown in the drawing. "Weave" the strips together by lifting the flaps up and over on both sides. Machine baste together 5/8 inch away from the left edge, catching all raw edges of the points in the seam.

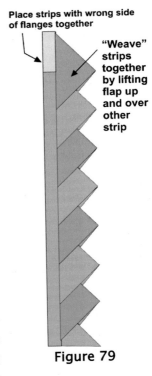

Figure 79

An example of prairie points on the inside of a binding is shown in Figure 80. Here two strips of prairie points were overlapped but not woven together. A separate small prairie point was added in the corner.

The prairie point strip is attached to the front of the quilt just like any other embellishment, described in EB5 below. Trim the flange to the width of your seam allowance, making sure all stitching and raw edges will be hidden within the seam. Pin the strips carefully in place and machine baste before putting on the binding.

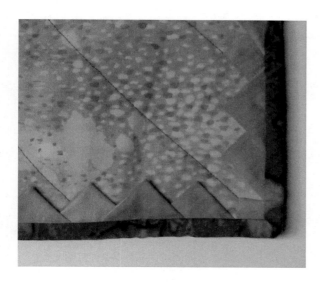

Figure 80

EB5. Contrasting Trim

Add a contrasting trim such as a flange, piping, rick rack, lace, or prairie points. All of these can be attached at the inside edge of a double fold binding. Before showing how to attach these trims we will look at some examples.

Figure 81 shows a piped binding.

Figure 81

Purchased lace can be used as shown in Figure 82.

Figure 82

Another possible embellishment is rick rack. Figure 83 shows a variegated purchased rick rack integrated into binding.

Figure 83

And as described earlier and shown in Figure 80, prairie points can be used on the inside of the binding.

There are two methods for attaching the binding after the trim is in place. The first method described below in EB5A is an "all stitching by machine" method. The second method, described later in EB6, is the more conventional first side by machine, second side by hand, stitching method.

After attachment of the trim, and before application of the binding, the quilt will look as shown in Figure 84. When adding a trim to the inside edge of the binding, the technique is the same for all trims.

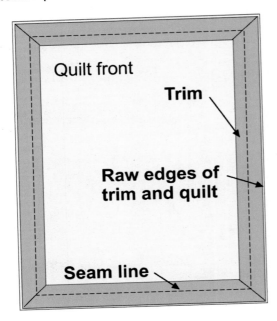

Figure 84

EB5A.   <u>Decide how wide you want the binding to be.</u> Machine baste a short piece of the trim to your quilt sandwich just inside the seam allowance. Follow the instructions for making a test sample in step 1 and adjust the binding width and/or the trim position until you are satisfied. The piping or trim adds some bulk to the

outside edge, so you might need a slightly wider binding strip than for a plain edge. Remember that the corners will be the bulkiest, so make allowances for them by being generous with the width. "Generous" is probably adding an additional 1/8th inch to the cut width of the binding strips.

Remove the test sample.

NOTE: For attachment completely by machine, you will still attach the trim on the front of the quilt but you will attach the binding to the back side first, then turn it over and attach the folded edge on top of the trim on the front.

EB5B. <u>Sew trim to quilt sandwich</u>. Once you have decided the right width for your binding and the placement of your trim, attach the trim to your quilt sandwich, with the raw edges along the outside raw edges of your quilt sandwich. Depending on the width of the trim, its raw edges may or may not line up with the outside edge of the quilt. If it is wider than the binding seam allowance, cut it to the seam allowance width before applying. If it is narrower than the binding seam allowance, make it extend into the seam allowance enough to be firmly attached (at least 1/8th inch).

If the trim is very narrow, you may bend it at the corners and attach one long piece; but more likely you will need to attach four pieces, one on each edge of the quilt. If your trim has an irregular edge or a pattern, match the pattern at the corners and create

44

a seam in the center of each edge at a place where the joining of the pattern will be least conspicuous. The trim can be overlapped at the corners as shown in Figure 85, or some trims will look better turned under to create a mitered corner as shown in Figure 86.

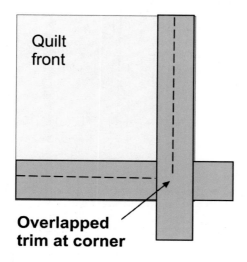

Figure 85

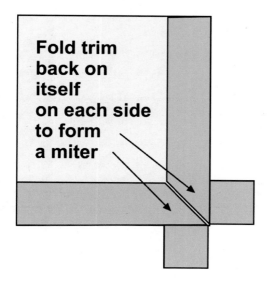

Figure 86

EB5C. Piping. Measure the perimeter of your quilt, and cut enough bias strips of fabric 1

½ inches wide to cover the measurement plus 10-20 inches extra length.

Join the strips on the diagonal the same way you did for binding in steps 4 through 6 on pages 6-7 as needed to create four strips the lengths of the edges of your quilt. Press the strips in half lengthwise, wrong sides together. These strips can be used without piping inserted to make an accent flange, or can be filled with cording.

The technique for making piping is described in section EB3 on page 34.

Stitch the cording into the piping for all four sides of your quilt, following the instructions in EB3. Use a thread color that matches your piping fabric. Trim the piping seam allowance to ¼ inch.

EB5D. Sew the piping to each edge of your quilt by the same method used for other trims, as described above in EB5 on page 43. Use a bobbin thread color that contrasts with the back of your quilt. Decide whether to overlap the corners or miter them. You may wish to cut the cording (not the piping fabric!) at the corner to minimize bulk. If so, remove the stitching from the piping back to the corner, cut the cording off there, and then restitch the piping.

NOTE: A consistent seam allowance for this piping application is very important. Stitch slowly and carefully. Check your result when finished, and correct any mistakes.

EB5E. After the piping or other trim is fully attached, prepare the binding. With the right width determined, cut and join your binding strips as in steps 4 through 6 on pages 6–7.

EB6A. All Machine Binding Application. Attach the binding to the back of the quilt first, following the instructions in Chapter III. Pay careful attention to the trim seam line and stitch a consistent seam that covers the trim seam line but does not cover the rest of the trim. Then attach the second side of the binding to the front of the quilt by following the instructions in Chapter IV, step 25B on page 17.

EB6B. "Second side by hand" method. We will generally follow the methods described in steps 7 through 21 on pages 9–13, but with one difference. This difference will make a big improvement in the appearance of narrow trims such as piping, so take the time to study this technique and master it. Once you understand it, it is no more difficult than regular binding.

We apply the binding to the front of the quilt, flipping and folding the corners, joining the ends, etc. The big difference is that the sewing will be done from the <u>back</u> of the quilt. With this method, the stitching line where you applied the trim is visible (remember that contrasting bobbin thread I told you to use?) and you will use it as a guide while applying the binding. The result will be a perfect seam line that lies just inside the piping/trim stitching.

So here's how you do it. Refer to Figure 87 to see how this works.

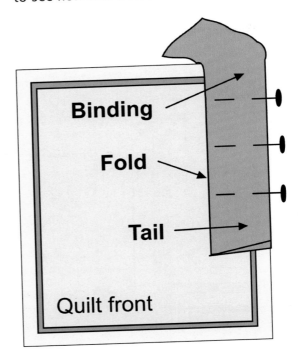

Figure 87

Position your binding to avoid putting joining seams in the corners, as described in step 7 on page 9. Lay the binding down on the front of the quilt, leaving a 10–12 inch tail that will not be stitched at this time. The binding will be laid down so that the binding goes around the quilt counterclockwise, as shown in Figure 87. Pin the binding in place as shown. When you turn the quilt over and stitch from the back, your stitching will be going clockwise, the "normal" direction, as shown in Figure 88.

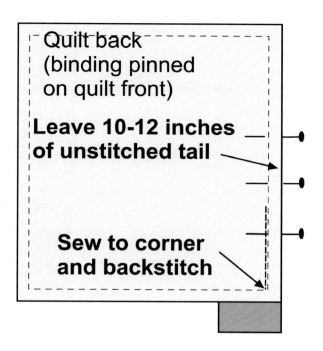

Quilt back
(binding pinned
on quilt front)

Leave 10-12 inches
of unstitched tail

Sew to corner
and backstitch

Figure 88

Turn the quilt over and line up the binding raw edge with the quilt raw edge. Put the quilt sandwich and binding under the presser foot of your sewing machine. If your piping or trim is very thick, you may want to use a zipper foot. Otherwise, a walking foot is the best choice.

Start sewing, just a hair inside the piping attachment stitching (that is, away from the raw edges). Consistent location of this stitching – very close to the piping stitching but just inside it – is the key to a great looking result. Sew to within a couple of inches of the corner, mark the diagonal corner, and then sew up to but not over your mark. Backstitch or sew off the edge. All these steps are exactly the same as if you were stitching from the front.

Remove the quilt from the machine and clip the threads. Turn the quilt over to the front and make a flip and fold corner. This is just the same as the normal method, except you are going counterclockwise. Make the fold directly in line with the piping/trim corner. Pin the fold down carefully, keeping the pins well away from the seam line area.

Turn the quilt to the back side and <u>carefully</u> slide the corner under the presser foot of your machine, making sure all the layers are properly lined up. Start sewing 3/8 inch away from the corner, backstitching to the seam allowance to lock the stitches. When you have sewed 12-15 inches past the corner, stop with the needle down. Test the corner you just made by folding it over to see if it will miter properly. Sometimes the piping adds enough bulk that the binding won't cover the seams in the corner. Now is the time to fix that problem, before you have sewn the rest of the binding down!

Continue sewing to the next corner, keeping the binding raw edges lined up with the quilt raw edges.

Repeat all the way around the quilt. Stop about 12 inches away from where you started sewing. Turn the quilt over and join the binding ends by the method described in steps 16 through 21 on pages 12-13.

Pin the joined binding down to the quilt front, but do the pinning from the quilt back. Sew the joined ends of the completed binding down, still staying just inside the piping attachment stitching.

Finish the binding on the back by hand, using the methods described in Chapter IV.

Figure 89 is the finished result – a close up view of a (nearly) perfect piped binding.

Figure 89

VII. Other Edge Treatments

You may wish to finish the quilt edge without a double fold binding. This may be for a placemat where the goal is a fast finish, an art quilt where the binding would detract from the visual impact of the piece, or where the edge is irregular. There are four categories of such edge treatments:

Self Binding. The back of the quilt is cut larger than the front and then folded over to the front, forming a self-binding.

Facing. The quilt edge is faced (a form of binding where the binding does not show on the front).

No-binding Turned Quilts. The edge is finished by sewing the back of the quilt to the front with right sides together, leaving a small hole to turn the whole thing right sides out. This is a common technique used for tied quilts, and is sometimes referred to as a "pillow" or "envelope" finish.

Single Fold Binding. A single fold binding eliminates the first lengthways press of the fabric, so the binding has only one layer of fabric. A single fold binding can be an excellent choice if you wish to bind each edge separately and miter the corners with seams, rather than using a continuous strip

of binding and the flip and fold technique.

SB. Self Binding

SB1. <u>Cut the quilt back 2 inches larger</u> than the front on all sides. Complete the quilting, leaving about 2 inches unquilted on the outer edges.

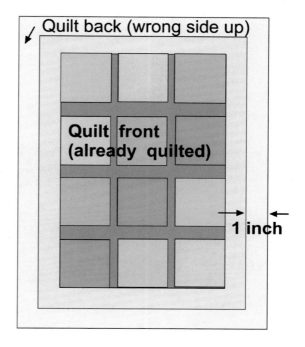

Figure 90

SB2. <u>Fold the excess backing fabric</u> out of the way (you may wish to hold it in place with painter's tape). Square up the quilt front edges. Unfold the quilt backing fabric and carefully trim it to 1 inch larger than the quilt top on all edges, as shown in Figure 90. Make it larger if you prefer.

You can finish the quilt edges with the folded method described here in SB3-SB6, or the corner seam method described below in SB7–SB11. Either method can be finished by hand or machine.

SB3. <u>Folded Method</u>. Test fold one corner of the quilt, following the steps below. If there is too much bulk in the corner, cut away a triangular piece (about the width of your first fold – probably ½ inch) in the corner as shown in Figure 91.

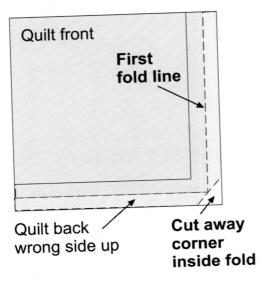

Figure 91

SB4. <u>Press a ½ inch hem</u> in one edge of the quilt backing, then fold ½ inch again over the quilt front as shown in Figure 92.

SB5. <u>Pin this edge in place</u>, taking care to have a consistent width. Miter the corner by folding the small triangle in the corner up before folding the next edge, as shown in Figure 93.

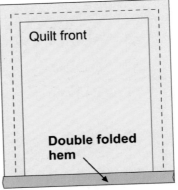

Press 1/2 inch hem in backing fabric; then fold 1/2 inch again onto quilt front

Figure 92

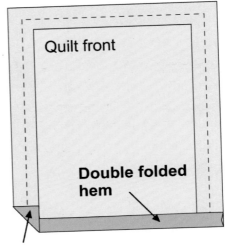

Figure 93

SB6. <u>Fold the second edge over twice</u>, pinning the mitered corner in place. Continue pinning the second quilt edge. When you reach the next corner, miter it in the same way. Continue on around the quilt. At the last corner, unfold the first edge just at the end, miter the corner as before, and then refold the first edge.

The completed folded edge is shown in Figure 94. Sew it in place with a blind hem stitch or use your sewing machine.

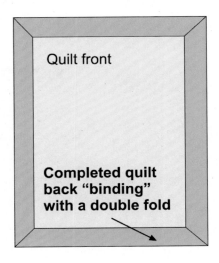

Quilt front

Completed quilt back "binding" with a double fold

Figure 94

Careful pressing and pinning are the keys to a good result for this type of finish.

SB7. <u>Corner Seam method</u>. These sewn-in corners eliminate some of the bulk. My sample piece here is a placemat with a flower print in the center, a mitered yellow border, and a wide self-binding in green. The top, batting, and backing pieces are shown in Figure 95. The backing piece is cut 2 inches larger on all sides for this example.

Sandwich the quilt as usual. Complete any quilting through all three layers, avoiding the edge area where the backing fabric will cover the top when folded over. After quilting, re-trim the edges of the backing fabric to ensure a consistent width.

Figure 95

Press a ½ inch fold in the outer edges of the backing fabric.

SB8. <u>Mark the seam at the corners</u> on the wrong side of the backing fabric, shown in Figure 96. Make a straight line across the corner, forming an accurate 45 degree triangle.

Figure 96

SB9. <u>Fold the quilt along the diagonal</u> (right side out) forming a point in the corner as shown in Figure 97. Pin the marked seam line, checking the back to ensure the seam lines match up. Also mark or pin a stopping point at the ½ inch fold.

Figure 97

Now sew the seam, starting at the corner diagonal fold and stopping with a backstitch at the hem fold point– ½ inch in this example. Then cut the point away as shown in Figure 98.

Figure 98

SB10. <u>Sew all four corner seams</u>, then press the corner seams open with your fingers. Fold the raw edges of the backing over the

front of the quilt, tucking the quilt corners inside the points. Use a point turner to get the points sharp, and use your fingers to open up the seam allowances inside so they lie flat. Fold and pin the hem under all around the quilt, as shown in Figure 99.

Figure 99

SB11. <u>Sew the folded hem edge</u> down on all four sides as shown in Figure 100. A straight stitch, decorative stitch or a zigzag stitch can be used.

Figure 100

QF. Quilt Facings

Two quilt facing techniques are presented here, both quick and easy. Block and square up your quilt before using either of these techniques. If your quilt allows it, use a ½ inch seam allowance instead of ¼ inch. It will be easier to turn and press the facing.

Turning the corner of a facing can be made easier by trimming out the bulk in the corner. One quick method is to fold back the quilt front and back fabrics and <u>cut the batting only</u> back to slightly inside the stitching line as shown in Figure 101.

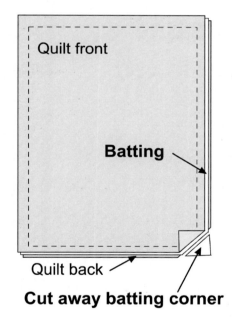

Cut away batting corner

Figure 101

QF1. <u>Continuous strip facing.</u>

QF1A. <u>Prepare a facing strip</u> the length of the perimeter of your quilt plus about 20 inches. The width of this strip is your choice. It can be a wide strip pressed in half lengthways, or a single layer of fabric.

The single layer will provide less bulk in the seam and make the corners slightly easier to turn.

For a single layer, I recommend a strip cut 2 ½ inches wide. Press under a ½ inch hem all along one edge.

For a double layer strip, I recommend cutting a 4 inch wide strip. Join as many strips as you need and then press in half along the entire length.

QF1B. <u>Lay the strip on the quilt front</u> (right sides together) with the raw edge of the facing lined up with the raw edge of the quilt. For the single layer version, this is the edge without the pressed hem.

Leave about a 10 inch unstitched tail. Start sewing with a 1/2 inch seam (unless you don't have enough space on the quilt edge; then use a ¼ inch seam). Stop sewing 2 inches from the corner, leaving the needle down. Mark the corner diagonal as in step 14 on page 11. Resume sewing and continue to the marked line. Turn the quilt and the facing strip 45 degrees; take one stitch along the diagonal, then turn another 45 degrees and line up with the next edge of the quilt, also lining up the facing strip with this edge.

NOTE: Because you are turning the whole facing to the back of the quilt, you do not need to do the "flip and fold" technique at the corner.

QF1C. <u>Continue sewing all the way around the quilt</u>, repeating the marking and turning process at each corner until you get about 12 inches away from the starting point. Stop sewing and join the facing ends using the same technique described in steps 16-20 on pages 12-13. Sew down the final section of facing as in step 21 on page 13.

QF1D. <u>Press the seam.</u> Press as sewn first to set; then carefully turn the seam allowance to the back of the quilt and press in place. This process may be made easier by trimming away bulk at the corners and grading the seam along each edge. Use a skewer or turning tool to push the corners out as square as possible.

NOTE: For this and the following facing technique, you can use a clothing construction technique called "understitching" that helps facings to lay flat. Open up the edge facing seam and press flat. Understitch the facing <u>to the seam allowance only</u> 1/16th inch away from the previous stitching line, holding the facing taut away from the quilt front. Go as close to the corners as you can, stopping at least 2 ½ inches before the corner to allow room for folding the mitered corner in the facing. Backstitch, lock the stitches, or pull the threads through to the seam allowance and knot them.

If you used a single layer of fabric for the facing, turn under the ½ inch hem and press again if desired.

QF1E. <u>Pin the hem edge of facing</u> to the back of the quilt, mitering each corner. Hand sew the hem edge to the quilt, being careful not to sew through to the quilt front.

QF2. <u>Four Strip Stitched Corner Facing.</u>

For this technique I am indebted to Jeri Riggs, at http://jeririggs.blogspot.com. There are many variations on this idea, but her clear description made the most sense to me. Kathleen Loomis has her own excellent version of this method I recently discovered. Her method greatly reduces the bulk in the corners, and is described fully in her blog at the following location: http://artwithaneedle.blogspot.com/2011/03/perfect-faced-quilts-tutorial.html

QF2A. <u>Square up the quilt</u> and measure the width and length. Cut four strips of fabric 2½ inches wide, slightly longer than the four sides of your quilt. Piece the strips as necessary for larger quilts.

QF2B. <u>Press under ¼ inch</u> along one long side of each strip as if you were making a hem. This could also be a ½ inch hem if you prefer.

QF2C. <u>Pick two sides</u> (I generally pick the top and bottom of the quilt) to be the edges with the sewn-in corners. Cut the two facing strips for these sides to be ¼ inch <u>shorter</u> than the quilt sides.

Place these first two facing strips right side down on the front of your quilt. The pressed-under raw edge will be facing up, shown in Figure 102.

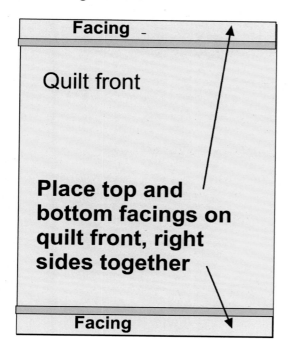

Figure 102

QF2D. <u>Start sewing</u> (with a ½ inch seam allowance if your quilt edge allows it, or ¼ inch seam if it doesn't) at one short side of the facing, leaving the ¼ inch "hem" loose. Measure and mark the corner so you know when you get there. Sew to the corner, turn and sew one diagonal stitch at the corner, then turn and continue sewing along the quilt edge. <u>Stretch the facing fabric slightly (or pin, if you prefer) so the facing strip end and the quilt side align when you get to the other end of the strip.</u> Turn the corner, again with one diagonal stitch, and finish at the hem fold as shown in Figure 103.

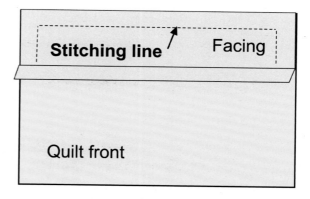

Figure 103

Complete the opposite side of the quilt the same way.

QF2E. <u>For the other two sides</u>, cut the facing strips about 2 inches <u>shorter</u> than the side measurement. Lay the facing strips right side down on the quilt top over the other two facing strips as shown in the detail in Figure 104.

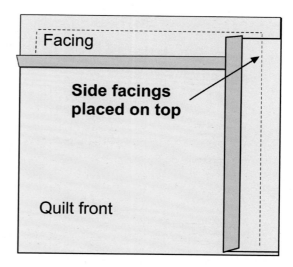

Figure 104

The shorter side strips must cover the turned "hem" of the top and bottom facings, but not extend into the corners where they would add bulk.

QF2F. <u>Sew the ¼ inch seam</u> on the side facings. Trim the bulk in the corners, turn and press in place. Hand sew the "hem" edge with a blind hem stitch (Figure 105).

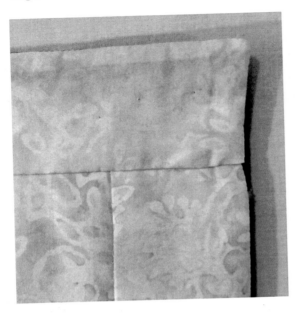

Figure 105

Figure 106

The facing will be hidden from the front. Figure 106 below shows the front of the quilt shown in Figure 105.

TQ. "No Binding" or Turned Quilts

These finishes vary from bare bones basic to lovely unusual finishes only limited by your imagination.   We'll start with the simplest and get more adventurous later.

TQ1. <u>Super fast "envelope" finish.</u> The quilt is tied rather than quilted or is quilted after turning.

TQ1A. <u>Square up the quilt top</u>.

TQ1B. <u>Layer the quilt sandwich</u> in the following order: batting on the bottom, quilt front (right side up) in the middle, quilt back (right side down) on top. Smooth each layer out carefully as you put it down.

Cut the batting and backing to the same dimensions as the quilt top.

TQ1C. <u>Pin all edges of the quilt.</u> Sew the layers together with a ¼ or ½ inch seam as desired, leaving an opening along one edge for turning. I mark this opening by pinning two pins close together at the stop point; the double pin reminds me to stop before I accidentally stitch the opening closed. The width of the opening must be big enough to get the whole quilt through it. This can be a 4-6 inch opening for a placemat, or a 12-18 inch opening for a large quilt. Backstitch as you start and stop at the opening. At each corner, turn halfway and take one diagonal stitch, then complete the turn.

TQ1D. <u>Check the entire edge for unwanted tucks or folds on the back side</u>. Rip out and re-sew as necessary. Cut the corners diagonally to remove bulk but leave 1/8 inch or so at the corner so the stitching will hold.

TQ1E. <u>Turn the quilt right side out through the opening</u>. Use a point turner to make the corners nice and neat. Be gentle to avoid pushing the point turner right through the seam. Press the edges of the quilt. Pin the opening closed, folding in the seam allowances. Sew by hand with a blind hem stitch; or, sew by machine with matching thread.

After the edge is completed, you can choose to tie or quilt your quilt. Quilting a turned quilt is a little tricky. It's not much

of a problem for something like a placemat with a stiff batting, but a lap-sized quilt with a fluffy batting will be very difficult to quilt without getting puckers on the back. Pin the quilt sandwich carefully and check that the back is smooth and taut before quilting.

TQ2. <u>Quilt before turning</u>. This is a good method for small quilts and wall hangings. The quilting is done on the quilt front and batting only. A few of the quilting lines can be reserved for sewing after the quilt is turned, to stabilize the back.

TQ2A. <u>Place the quilt front on top of the batting.</u> Pin together and quilt as desired. Square up the quilt and stitch a line of basting all the way around the quilt perimeter at ¼ inch. Use a thread for the bobbin that contrasts with your batting.

TQ2B. <u>Layer the quilt sandwich</u> with the backing fabric on the bottom right side up, then the quilted quilt front and batting on top, right side down. Smooth out all layers and pin carefully around the edge. Sew around the edge with the batting facing up. Use the ¼ inch basting stitch line as a reference; stitch just inside this line all the way around except at the opening left for turning.

TQ2C. <u>Check the back side for tucks or folds</u>. Clip out the bulk at the corners and clip or notch any curves. Turn the quilt right side out. Press the edges carefully, paying special attention to the corners. Pin under the seam allowances at the opening and close it by hand or machine stitching as you prefer.

Complete any quilting you reserved to stabilize the quilt back, and you are done!

One of the advantages of this technique is that there are lots of variations to add interest or functionality to your quilt. Here are a few possibilities:

TQ3. Add hanging tabs to the quilt top and decorative tabs to the quilt bottom. Add the tabs or trim after the top and batting have been quilted.

Place the tabs where you like. Machine baste the tabs in place on the quilt top. Then layer the quilt sandwich as above in step TQ2B. Sew the sandwich together, leaving an opening. Remove bulk from the corners, clip any curves. Turn right sides out, pressing carefully. Close the opening. An example of this technique is shown in Figure 107.

Figure 107

The decorative tabs at the bottom can be most anything you like – yarn, prairie points, ribbon, etc. Of course they can also be added to the sides of the quilt.

TQ4. Irregular quilt edges. No need to restrict yourself to a square quilt! Figure 108 shows a quilt from a great pattern called "Branching Out" by Random Threadz (website www.randomthreadz.com).

Figure 108

Figure 109

TQ5. Scallop edge with piping. As described in Chapter VI, Embellished Bindings, piping can be inserted into a regular binding. A simpler method is to add piping to the edge without binding. Figure 109 shows a small quilt with a piped and scalloped edge.

This unique edge treatment was accomplished in several ways. First, the dark navy "skirt" at the bottom is a separate piece, attached on the back of the main quilt by hand stitching after the main quilt was completed. The beads at the bottom were sewn on by hand as the last step.

The main quilt was pieced and appliquéd, then sandwiched with the batting and backing. It was sewn around the sides and bottom, and then turned leaving the entire top edge open. The quilting was completed. The top edge was finished with a conventional double fold binding, the ends tucked in and carefully hand stitched. The result is a lovely layered look that makes the quilt appear to have four layers, when it actually has two.

The piping is made from fabric cut on the bias and prepared as described in EB3 on page 34.

TQ5A. The borders on the quilt front are made square, larger than the scalloped edge. The curve for the location of the piping seam allowance is marked on the quilt top as shown in Figure 110.

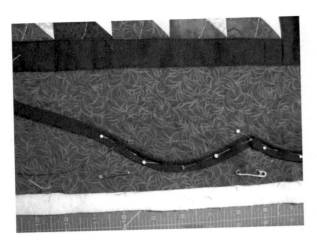

Figure 110

Here I used an iron-away black marker. The black line shows on the lower left of the photo. The piping has not yet been pinned down in this area.

TQ5B. <u>The piping is carefully pinned around the quilt perimeter</u>, with the piping seam allowance clipped at the inside corners. The bias fabric used for the piping allows the outside edge to stretch around the curves. When the piping is completely pinned, it is carefully sewn in place using a zipper foot, making sure the stitching lies just inside the stitching line on the piping itself. Figure 111 shows the piping completely applied. I have deliberately not trimmed the quilt along the curves yet; it is much easier to sew accurately if the presser foot has fabric all the way underneath it.

The cording used in this piping is narrow enough that the start and end of the piping were just overlapped and the ends pinned into the seam allowance.

Figure 111

A thicker cording would need to be cut out of the piping as described in EB3 on page 34 to eliminate bulk.

As in previous methods, the bobbin thread used to apply this piping contrasts with the quilt batting. This stitching line will be used as a reference when joining the quilt front and back.

TQ5C. <u>The quilt back was cut square</u> to match the quilt front shown in Figure 111. The quilt back is placed right side up and the quilt front placed on top, right side down. The two layers are pinned together around the edge. The layers are stitched together –I used my walking foot since the cording was thin and didn't add much of a ridge. A zipper foot could have been used to avoid the ridge made by the cording, but wasn't necessary here.

The sewing followed the piping attachment line and was just inside the piping stitching. This provides a very accurate seam and eliminates nearly all instances where exposed stitching from the piping construction must be ripped out at the end.

TQ5D. I left one of the corner scallops open for turning since it provided the longest edge without an inside corner. Before turning right side out, the seam was carefully cut to ¼ inch, graded, clipped at the inside corners and notched along the curved edges. This clipping and notching is essential to getting a nice smooth edge. Then the quilt was turned right side out. The edges were pressed down so they lay smooth and flat before the opening was closed, since some more trimming might have been necessary. The opening was hand sewn closed on the back of the quilt.

The resulting quilt is shown in Figure 109 on page 59.

Single Fold Binding.

Single fold bindings can be more difficult than double fold bindings when applied using the flip and fold method. If you plan to apply your binding to each quilt edge separately and use seamed mitered corners, single fold binding may be a better choice. The single layer results in much less bulk in the corner seams.

An excellent single fold binding technique called Seamless Quilt Bindings has been developed by Dena Crain. Dena describes this technique very thoroughly on her website at the following link: http://www.denacrain.com/blog/tutorials/seamless-quilt-binding/. The photo in Figure 112 shows one of my quilts using her method. The single layer of fabric makes the corners neat and not bulky. This method is especially suitable for quilts entered in competitions, where mitered corners like this are much appreciated by judges.

Figure 112

VIII. Conclusion

I hope the techniques in this book help you make beautiful bindings, and that you are inspired to add interest to your quilts with some of the suggested variations.

The edge treatments you use are limited only by your imagination. The books, articles, and websites listed in Chapter VIV provide more ideas and can add to your knowledge and skills.

For you traditional quilters, I highly recommend "A Fine Finish: New Bindings for Award Winning Quilts" by Cody Mazuran   (Reference 1). Her bindings are wonderful on traditional quilts for the quilter who has the time and the desire for heirloom quality results.   If you have devoted countless hours to making an heirloom quilt, it only makes sense to bind it appropriately.

VIV. References

1. **A Fine Finish: New Bindings for Award-Winning Quilts** by Cody Mazuran 1996, 2007 by That Patchwork Place. Available at www.martingale-pub.com.

2. **Happy Endings - Finishing The Edges of Your Quilt** by Mimi Dietrich 1987, 2011 by That Patchwork Place. Available at www.martingale-pub.com.

3. **Binding Basics and Beyond** by the editors of Quilters Newsletter and Quiltmaker magazines, 1996, Leman Publications, Inc.

4. **American Quilter**™ magazine articles - available to members of American Quilters Society online at www.americanquilter.com

    a. **Crowning Glory for Quilts: Perfectly Piped Bindings** by Susan K. Cleveland, Winter 2005 pages 20-24

    b. **Face It!: A Better Quilt Edge** by Kathleen Loomis, Projects 2007, pages 82-85

    c. **A Slim Finish: Narrow Bindings for Miniatures and Small Projects** by Marci Baker, Winter 2006.

    d. **Yes, A Yarn Binding** by Wendy Butler Berns, Projects 2006 pages 32-33

    e. **Faux Piped Binding** by Trisha Chubbs, September 2012, page 60

    f. **Precision-Pieced Binding** by Barbara M. Burnham, November 2012, page 62

5. **French Twist Binding** by Gretchen Hudock, Quilters Newsletter magazine, September 2001.

6. **Finish With A Flourish** by Sherri Bain Driver, Quiltmaker magazine 2002

7. **Piping Hot Binding** by Susan K Cleveland, 2008. Available online at Susan's website, www.PiecesBeWithYou.com

8. **QUILTapestry Orphan Block Rescue** by Helle-May Cheney, published in The Quilting Quarterly Winter 2012, The Journal of the National Quilting Association.

9. Online sources - these tend to change rapidly, but were available at the time of this writing.

    a. for some great non-binding finish alternatives, check out Brenda Gael Smith's website where on her blog she has summarized several web-based tutorials found in a search: http://serendipitypatchwork.com.au/blog/2008/02/04/free-non-binding-alternative-quilt-finishes/ .

    b. **Seamless Quilt Bindings** by Dena Crain, located on her website at the following address: http://www.denacrain.com/blog/tutorials/seamless-quilt-binding/ .

    c. **Perfect Faced Quilts Tutotial** by Kathleen Loomis, located on her website at the following address: http://artwithaneedle.blogspot.com/2011/03/perfect-faced-quilts-tutorial.html

Additional copies of this book can be purchased at:

www.createspace.com/3959581

or through www.amazon.com

If you have comments or suggestions for this book, please write to the author at:

valleyview@olypen.com

65491192R00042

Made in the USA
San Bernardino, CA
02 January 2018